CITY CHICKENS

BY CHRISTINE HEPPERMANN

Houghton Mifflin Books for Children

HOUGHTON MIFFLIN HARCOURT

Boston   New York   2012

Houghton Mifflin Books for Children is an imprint of Houghton Mifflin Harcourt Publishing Company.

www.hmhbooks.com

The text of this book is set in Chaparral Pro.

Photo credits:
pages 2, 3 (top), 4 (top and middle), 5, 6, 7, 8 (bottom), 11 (top left), 16, 17, 18 (left), 20 (bottom), 23 (left and bottom right), 24, 26, 28 (bottom right), 29, 31, 33, 34, 35, 38, 39, 45 (right), 48 (bottom), 49, 51 (left): Eric Hinsdale
pages 3 (bottom), 8 (top), 9, 10, 11 (bottom left), 13, 14, 15, 18 (right), 19, 20 (top), 23 (top right), 28 (top left and bottom left), 34 (top), 37, 41, 44, 45 (left), 47, 48 (top left, top center, and top right), 50, 51 (right), 52: Mary Britton Clouse
page 4 (bottom): Ruth Lais
page 11 (top right): Cynthia Porter
page 22 (top): Mercy for Animals
page 22 (bottom): David Harp Courtesy United Poultry Concerns
page 43: Katie Young

Library of Congress Cataloging-in-Publication Data
Heppermann, Christine.
  City chickens / by Christine Heppermann.
     p. cm.
  ISBN 978-0-547-51830-5
1. Chickens—Minnesota—Anecdotes. 2. Animal welfare—Minnesota—Anecdotes. 3. Animal shelters—Minnesota—Anecdotes. I. Title.
  SF487.8.M5H47 2012
  636.509776—dc22
  2011009754

Manufactured in China
LEO 10 9 8 7 6 5 4 3 2 1
4500340327

FOR MARY AND BERT. AND FOR MY
FLOCK—ERIC, CLAUDIA, AND AUDREY.

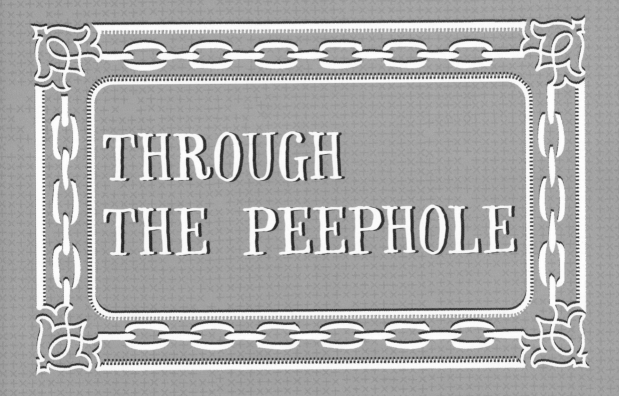

THROUGH THE PEEPHOLE

A bus roars down Lowry Avenue.

A dog howls along with a fire truck siren.

Jump ropes swish against the pavement.

A rooster crows.

If you happened to be out walking in this busy North Minneapolis, Minnesota, neighborhood, you might wonder, *Did I really* hear *what I think I just heard? A rooster? In the middle of the city?*

There's the sound again!

Follow it to the pinkish-brown stucco house on the corner........

The house belongs to Mary Britton Clouse and her husband, Bert. Walk around to the weathered wooden fence that surrounds Mary and Bert's backyard.

Halfway down the west side of the fence hangs a faded painting of a chicken with flowing white tail feathers.

Tug on the painting and it swings sideways, revealing a peephole........

Look through the peephole to discover a place like no other—an inner-city animal shelter called Chicken Run Rescue.

At this shelter, no dogs or cats wait in cages for people to fall in love with them and give them homes. These "guests," as Mary and Bert call them, wear feathers, not fur. And though they spend their nights in cages, during the day they are everywhere.

In the garden, taking dust baths.
In the kitchen, eating spaghetti.
In the living room, laying eggs under the couch.
In a playpen in the dining room, recovering from an illness.
In the second-floor bathroom, nesting in the shower stall.
In the house and in the yard, upstairs and downstairs, on a bench or a perch, on top of a table or beside it, crowing.

Yet at Chicken Run Rescue, as at any other animal shelter, people *do* fall in love.

Chickens roll in the dirt to remove oil, dead skin, and insects such as mites, and to help keep their feathers strong and shiny.

Someone has been busy in the living room.

Pierce the rooster has a quiet place to rest and get better.

Coraline the hen contemplates a snack.

Getting to know one of the birds up for adoption.

Mary Britton Clouse falls in love every time she drives to Minneapolis Animal Control or one of the local Humane Society shelters to pick up another guest.

She gently places the scared rooster or hen in a pet carrier lined with a soft swatch cut from an old bedspread and says, "Let's go, sweetheart. Your life is about to change."

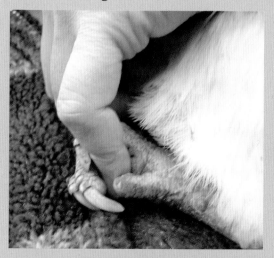

Hand in Hand/Self-Portrait.

Safe in Mary's arms.

OFF THE FARM, INTO THE PARKING GARAGE

Where do these city chickens come from?

Sometimes it's a mystery. Animal Control officers have found chickens wandering in city parks, alleys, or even downtown parking garages. Perhaps the birds escaped from live poultry markets or backyard coops, which are legal and growing in popularity in both Minneapolis and its neighboring "twin" city, St. Paul. Callers to Animal Control have reported chickens eating from their wild bird feeders. One call directed officers to a rooster and hen left out in a cage by the curb with the garbage.

Ranger was resucued after police shut down a cockfighting operation in Minneapolis.

Some of Chicken Run Rescue's guests start life as cockfighting birds. Cockfighting is an illegal sport in which two roosters are forced into a ring, like a boxing ring, to attack one another until the loser is either too injured to continue or dead from his wounds.

Others emerge from their shells in school classrooms during hatching projects. Students watch excitedly through incubator glass as chicks peck their way into the world. The babies are so cute and fluffy—and, all too often, homeless after the project ends, when a teacher or parent drops them off at a city shelter.

Most of the time Mary doesn't know a guest's whole story, and she doesn't care. She may not even be able to tell the bird's breed. But it never matters to her whether a chicken is an Araucana or an Australorp, a Jersey giant or a Rhode Island red. She just knows they need help.

"Chickens are the most abused, exploited animals on the planet," she explains. "They are the ones who need friends the most"

In summer, Mary's and Bert's backyard is green and inviting.

Tying chickens to a fence or object in the yard is a cruel way to keep them without having to provide shelter.

Chicks rescued from a roadside ditch.

THE HATCHING OF CHICKEN RUN RESCUE

As a little girl in upstate New York, Mary felt sure she was part dog. She believed she could hear and smell almost as well as her dog Dukie. Dukie was part German shepherd, part Labrador retriever, so she figured she must be "part" something, too.

She also loved to draw—mostly pictures of dogs. Mostly pictures of Dukie.

When she was six years old, her parents took her to a county fair and gave her a quarter for the "freak show." She remembers, "There was a miniature pony with a dirty, tangled mane standing inside a stinky stall." Though she doesn't recall any of the other exhibits she saw that day, the pony made a lasting impression. "I still tear up when I think of his sad eyes peering through the darkness at me."

After high school, Mary moved to Albuquerque, New Mexico, to study art. At art school she met Bert Clouse.

Bert grew up hunting and fishing in the Black Hills of South Dakota until something happened that made him decide to give away his guns and gear.

Mary and her dog Dukie.

Mary and friends on the front steps of her apartment in Albuquerque.

He says, "One beautiful, cool summer evening, friends and I were hanging out enjoying the sunset, taking turns trying to shoot a chipmunk that was sitting on a mound of dirt. When it was my turn, I shot her, no big deal. But the more I thought about it, my evening was ruined. So was the chipmunk's. I remember thinking she was just hanging out, like us, enjoying a summer evening. Something she would never do again."

Mary and Bert lived in the same apartment complex in Albuquerque. He says Mary was never afraid to "get in anybody's face" when she saw an animal being mistreated. A mother dog and puppies lived in the apartment alleyway, and Mary regularly brought them food and water. She convinced Bert to take in a stray kitten, which he named Gerhard.

Bert and his childhood dog Sandy.

"Gerhard became my constant companion, and, a few years later, so did Mary," Bert says.

A job for Bert at a printing company brought the couple to Minneapolis.

Mary restores old maps for a client.

The parakeet pen.

The backyard before...

They bought a house on the north side of town and eventually started an in-home business, repairing and restoring old books and papers for libraries across the country.

Marco, one of Mary and Bert's rescued dogs.

They also started taking in "throw-away" animals: first a dog, then two cats, then another dog, then birds—doves and parakeets whose former owners had decided that trills, chirps, and coos were just headache-making noise. Before long, Mary and Bert had an avian choir trilling, chirping, and cooing in a sunny pen on their back porch.

How did they go from helping dogs, cats, and pet birds to helping chickens?

. . and after .

It started with thirteen Thai roosters.

A friend at Animal Control told Mary about these tall, beautiful, regal birds, impounded after a cockfighting bust. Seven of the roosters were severely injured and had to be euthanized—killed. The remaining six had nowhere to go. Who would want them? Animal Control planned to euthanize them, too.

Mary refused to let that happen. She posted notices on the Internet and eventually found homes on nearby farms for the surviving Thai roosters.

In the meantime, she learned that Minneapolis Animal Control impounded more than fifty birds a year, and that three-quarters of those birds were chickens.

"If someone needs help, Mary just acts," Bert says. In contrast, he prefers to mull things over for a while, considering all the potential problems. But in 2001, when she told him she wanted to turn their inner-city house into a shelter for chickens, he trusted her passion and conviction.

So he and Mary got busy.

They set up chain-link pens and built sturdy, insulated wooden coops in their backyard, basement, and garage.

They went to a feed store and hefted fifty-pound bags of pellets and jumbo

Hens headed down to the basement for bed.

Hoping Bert turns over a worm.

An inviting home for new guests.

packages of wood shavings into shopping carts.

They applied for a special permit from the city, allowing them to keep up to fifteen chickens at a time. (This number later increased to twenty.)

They told Animal Control and area Humane Society shelters that they wanted to be notified about any impounded chickens.

They waited.
They didn't have to wait long.
Soon the first call came.

At the Animal Control shelter, Mary talked in soothing tones to a thin, ghost-white hen with patchy feathers. She brought her back to the stucco house, which now had a name: Chicken Run Rescue.

The first guest.

Mary gave the hen a name—Henrietta. Henrietta was Chicken Run Rescue's first guest. Mary never got the chance to handle the Thai roosters—they went straight from Animal Control to their new homes—so Henrietta was also the first chicken Mary ever held.

Stroking Henrietta's soft feathers, quieting her nervous clucks, Mary Britton Clouse knew what she wanted to do for the rest of her life.

Henrietta poses for Mary.

Like a mother hen, she would open her wings and protect every chicken she could.

Mary makes a guest feel at home.

UNEQUAL TREATMENT

It doesn't seem fair.

People give dogs pillowy beds, crunchy dog biscuits, big yards, long walks, even sweaters and booties. Cats get their heads scratched, their fur brushed. They play with catnip toys, eat gourmet tuna dinners, curl on cozy chairs to nap.

What do chickens get?

Mary's heart aches when she thinks about the more than eight billion chickens raised for food in the United States every year—more than all the cows, pigs, and sheep put together. Most spend their short lives on large commercial farms. These farms are sometimes called "factory farms" because they produce poultry in a way that treats the birds like objects rather than living beings.

Broilers, chickens raised for meat, live crowded together by the thousands on the floors of windowless sheds. They have to scramble over each other's backs just to reach their food. Layers, hens raised for eggs, are often crammed into cages stacked one atop the other, with no room to spread their wings, barely enough room to turn around. They stand all day on wire mesh floors that slice into their delicate feet.

There are no mesh floors at Chicken Run Rescue. The birds nest in soft piles of hay, dried leaves, or curled wood shavings. On commercial farms, chick-

Egg layer hens in a factory farm.

Jammed together in a space about the same size as a sheet of paper, the hens get agitated and peck off each other's feathers.

ens likely never go outdoors. At Chicken Run Rescue they dig in the dirt, perch on branches, sprawl in the grass to soak up sun through their wings. They don't eat only dry chicken feed.

They eat worms, tomatoes, romaine lettuce, cooked noodles, watermelon, grapes, oranges, raisins, and other tasty treats. If they jump into a lap, they get their heads scratched.

And, like dogs and cats and other companion animals, they all get names.

There's McNamara, a reddish-brown and black rooster with arthritis in his knees and feet. He sleeps on his back instead of on a perch the way most

chickens do, because he cleverly figured out that this position relieves the pressure from his aching joints.

There's Coraline, a small, mischievous black hen who seems to be everywhere at once—flapping up to sit in the windowsill, dashing off to investigate what all the squawking is about in the garden. Wherever the action is, Coraline is there.

There's Hilary, a smoky gray Thai hen, used in the past for breeding by a cockfighting operation. When she first came to Chicken Run Rescue, Hilary was

McNamara invents a new way to sleep.

Snacktime in the backyard.

Coraline checks in on the parakeets.

understandably frightened of people. Now she loves being held and will sometimes, Mary says, "burst into a skip for the joy of being free in the garden."

There's Fetzer, a wheat-colored rooster, Mary's helpmate for evening chores. She says, "He patrols the yard and manages to rearrange the pile of leaves and straw I've just swept up." He also loves chasing squirrels and sparrows away from his food bowl.

There's Bing, Gody, Claude, Lotus,

Hannah, Raymond, Tara, Kandinsky— literally hundreds of birds who have passed through Chicken Run Rescue over the years.

When guests are ready—some birds with long-term health issues live at Chicken Run Rescue permanently— they move on to homes where they will receive the same kind of loving treatment Mary and Bert gave them. Homes where they aren't valued for their meat or their eggs, but for who they are.

A ROOSTER'S TALE

Billiam probes his beak into a juicy ants' nest. Always the gentleman, he doesn't keep his find to himself. Instead, he bobs his head and clucks rapidly, typical rooster talk for, "Hey, ladies, get over here. Food!"

As hens Jubilee and Butterscotch race toward him, he topples over on his side—not typical rooster behavior. Billiam often falls down when he's excited.

"Billy's an unusual guy," his "mom," Charlene Tallen, freely admits. His clumsiness is part of his unique charm, but it's also a reminder—along with his comb, shrunken by frost-bite—of his rough past. Now two years old, he is the quirky leader of the flock on the Tallen fam-ily's twenty-four-acre suburban Minneapolis hobby farm, peacefully sharing barn and pasture space with rescued horses, two dogs, and a ragtag bunch of cats.

Charlene's twelve-year-old daughter, Alison, adores Billiam, calling him "sweet, cute, and awesome."

Yet without Chicken Run Rescue, he never would have made it to the Tal-lens' farm. He probably would not be alive at all.

Billiam poses for his closeup.

Billiam is a popular guy on the Tallen farm.

DUMPED IN A DITCH

In Winona, Minnesota, on the cold, rainy night of April 6, 2008, drivers on Highway 14 might have mistaken the yellow clumps by the side of the road for early spring wildflowers or maybe scattered trash.

Eventually somebody noticed that the clumps were moving, that they were actually baby chickens. Lots of them.

Winona police officers Eric Mueller and Paul Anderson arrived near the Knopp Valley Drive entrance ramp to find damp chicks huddling together in a roadside ditch, with some chicks starting to wander off toward a line of trees. They also found empty boxes, apparently used to transport the chicks to their odd, hazardous location. The officers, along with passersby who'd stopped to help, grabbed the boxes and began filling them. When they'd finished, the squad car held 106 peeping passengers, ready for a late-night trip to the Winona Area Humane Society.

Humane Society workers, roused from their beds to open the shelter, along with the officers, acted quickly to help the chicks' delicate bodies recover from the cold. They spent the rest of the night warming the babies with heat lamps and towels. The feed store was closed, so they made do with what food they had on hand—a box of grits somebody grabbed from a home cupboard, and granulated sugar.

"I sat there on the floor of the Humane Society . . . dipping little beaks in sugar water," Officer Mueller told a reporter from the local paper the next day.

By morning, all but one of the chicks had survived and were contained in plastic children's wading pools normally reserved for dogs to splash in on

Billiam and his buddies.

Billiam relaxes in his bed in the Talen family's barn.

Chickens are commonly used in lab experiments.

hot days. Somewhere amid the crowd, perhaps pecking grits off a paper plate or snuggling against one of the stuffed animals that workers had placed in the pool to give it structure, was Billiam.

Police had solved the mystery of where the chicks came from, though they still didn't know who dumped them.

A biology lab at nearby St. Mary's University had ordered the birds for use in an experiment, which involved regularly injecting the chicks, all roosters, with the hormone testosterone and observing their growth and behavior. A biology student checked on the roosters around nine p.m. Sunday night. Police believed that the thieves entered the unlocked lab shortly thereafter.

St. Mary's did not want the chicks back. Removing them from the "controlled laboratory setting" ruined the experiment, a university spokesman explained.

Billiam and his brothers couldn't stay at the Humane Society shelter forever. Where could they go?

TO THE RESCUE

"It started with a phone call. I've had so many like it," Mary says.

Except this phone call was, in a way, different. Usually callers need help with one, maybe two chickens. This one needed help with 105.

Melissa Fogarty, a volunteer at the Winona Area Humane Society, learned about Chicken Run Rescue through another animal shelter she'd called for advice.

"We're a dog and cat shelter," Melissa told Mary. "We really don't have room to keep chickens."

Mary and Bert didn't have room at their house either. Even if they did, their permit would not allow them to take in that many guests at once.

Still, Mary had to do something.

"Things could go terribly wrong for these birds, and I could keep that from happening."

She assured Melissa that she had a long list of potential adopters and would start right away trying to find homes for the Winonas, as she and Bert came to call them.

This was before Melissa informed Mary that all of the chicks were roosters.

Hens are much easier to find homes for than roosters.

A SAD FACT

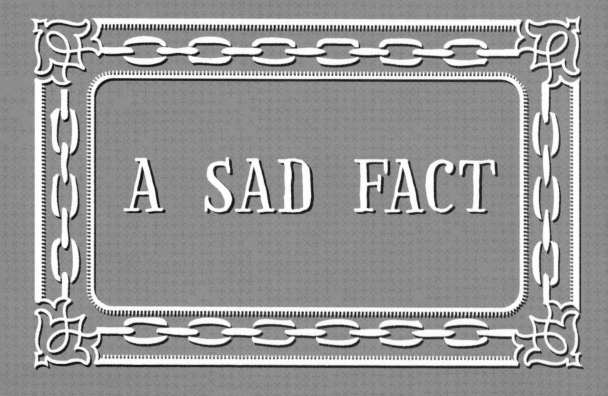

Most people who want chickens do not want roosters.

Chicken Run Rescue has sheltered many roosters over the years—too many, Mary and Bert would say. It's difficult to determine a baby chicken's sex, and roosters are frequently abandoned by owners who brought them home thinking they were hens, until they started crowing.

A rooster checks out one of the enclosures.

Roosters crow at any time of day, not just at sunrise. Yet no one has ever filed a noise complaint against Chicken Run Rescue.

Neighborhood children actually enjoy walking past Mary and Bert's backyard and being able to identify a rooster by his unique crow.

Some crows sound scratchy. Some sound high and clear, like trumpet solos. Some sound fog horn low.

Roosters have a reputation for aggression, and they will act fiercely to protect their flock from danger. But much of the time, as Mary has discovered, an aggressive rooster is a fearful one.

Guests who have suffered cruel treatment in the past panic and lash out because they assume humans intend to hurt them.

The oldest member of Chicken Run Rescue's permanent flock is a calm iridescent black rooster named Roseman. Roseman arrived at Chicken Run Rescue with a fractured leg and now walks with a limp, like an old pirate. He and Mary didn't always get along well. She wore thick canvas gloves when handling him, as he had a tendency to dig his beak into her wrist. By being patient and gentle, she slowly earned his trust.

These days Roseman eats raisins straight from Mary's gloveless hands, and Mary has learned that even the most fearful, damaged birds will change their behavior once they understand that they are in a safe place.

Farmers and backyard flock owners commonly dislike roosters for what they *don't* do—lay eggs. Thus, roosters are considered to be of little use, except in the stew pot. At hatcheries, the chicken-breeding operations that supply poultry farms with stock, most male chicks—a quarter of a billion each year—are killed soon after they are born.

Mary and Bert work to change people's minds about roosters. But could they change enough minds in time to help the 105 Winona chicks find homes?

Roosters stick close to hens to guard them from danger.

Fetzer announces his presence.

Mary and
Roseman: good
friends.

BILLIAM
GROWS UP

A feather duster dangles upside down on a wire above a rubber dishwashing bin. Through its gray plumage pokes a tiny yellow head, then another. Billiam and his brother Shiah like to hide beneath their substitute mom's "wings," where they feel safe—and they are safe. They and four other Winona chicks—Sketchy, Toe Joe, Steve, and Cindy Sidney (possibly a hen)—have arrived at Chicken Run Rescue.

Mary and Bert drove two hours to the Winona shelter, scooped the 102 chicks (three had been adopted by a Winona family) into four plastic pet carriers, and transported them to their friend Tracie's farm for temporary care. While unloading at the farm, they noticed a black toe on one of the chicks. Altogether, five of the Winonas had black toes, and a sixth couldn't stand properly. They brought the six chicks home with them to have them looked at by a veterinarian.

Veterinary care is expensive, and not every vet, especially in the city, accepts chickens as patients. But Mary and Bert believe that part of the responsibility of keeping an animal is giving it good medical care. They spend thousands of dollars every year on avian (bird) medications and office visits with the small number of local veterinarians willing and eager to work with creatures other than the usual dogs and cats.

Dr. Cynthia Fetzer determined that the black toes resulted from frostbite contracted during that cold night in the ditch. Eventually the blackened dead tissue would fall off, leaving the chickens still able to move about normally on their healthy toes. In the meantime, Mary and Bert needed to soak ten

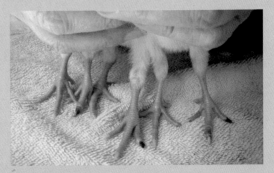

Toes blackened by frostbite.

Dr. Cynthia Fetzer, a north Minneapolis veterinarian, frequently provides care for Chicken Run rescue's guests.

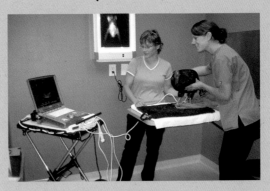

Roseman gets an ultrasound.

little feet in a solution of warm water and blue disinfectant twice a day to ward off infection.

Dr. Fetzer couldn't tell exactly why the sixth chick, now named Billiam after a nickname for Mary's older brother, wobbled.

Maybe he'd suffered a head injury in the lab or when dumped by the thieves. Maybe he was born that way.

Mary and Bert would watch him carefully and hope for the best.

The main way that Mary gets the word out about guests up for adoption is through a newsletter she calls "The Adoption Chronicles." She e-mails it to confirmed "chicken friends" who have signed up for her mailing list because they might want to adopt. Here's how, in the April 2008 newsletter, she introduced Billiam:

> Billiam Winona is our 301st rescue. He is an adolescent male Delaware [breed], pure white with soft gray and black specks on wings tail and neck. He is soft and gentle and stunningly beautiful. . . . Although he likes to belly bump with his brothers, he has been living with them happily since he was a week old. They are all very tame and run as a group to greet us, especially when they see the shiny treat bowl. They are still peeping but have been acclimated to living outdoors. They can fly really well. They will be thrilled to explore somebody's garden and meet a new flock.

Mary also posted Billiam's profile on Petfinder.com, a resource that lists adoptable animals nationwide.

In early June, Charlene Tallen and her then ten-year-old daughter, Alison, browsed Petfinder hoping to find a replacement for their rooster Little Richard, killed by a neighbor's dog.

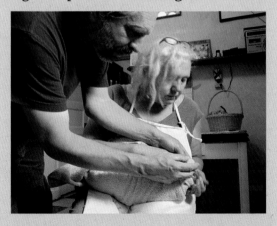

Mary holds the patient while Bert gives antibiotics with a syringe.

They stumbled on Mary's profile of Billiam.
They started reading.
They started falling in love.

BILLIAM GOES HOME

"**W**ho can't fall in love with Billy?" Charlene says today. "When he first came here, he would have seizures a lot and was very weak. He didn't crow. After a while of walking around and living the high life, he got stronger and started to crow. Now he crows all the time."

Billiam is loud, friendly, goofy, and clumsy. He's also tough.

He has survived two fox attacks on the Tallen flock. Charlene believes his seizures saved him, that all his frenzied flopping must have led the fox to choose different birds.

He survived a fight with another rooster that left him blind in one eye. Now Charlene and Alison give him eye drops every night.

They used to give him pills, too, for an upper respiratory infection, but he survived that, bunking in the Tallens' warm barn office for the winter, where he cozied up to the dogs and numerous barn cats.

Sketchy, Toe Joe, and the other Winonas at Chicken Run Rescue also survived and found permanent homes. Not all of their brothers on Tracie's farm were as fortunate. Mary and Bert tried their best, but, really, there just aren't enough people willing to take in roosters. As the birds grew bigger, Tracie had little choice but to let them out of their increasingly too-small pen to roam the pastures and woods. Big white roosters can't easily hide from predators. Fewer and fewer of them came back to the coop to roost every night. Tracie finally gave the remaining dozen or so Winonas to friends on a neighboring farm who had more space and were better equipped to shelter them.

As for Billiam, Charlene reports, "He is hanging out with his new group of girls. He is the boss, as best he can be. How he has survived all of his challenges, I'll never know. He just has some seriously great karma."

And, most important, he has a family who loves him.

Billiam goes for a walk.

Billiam and Alison.

CITY
CHICKENS

Katie Young can't leave homemade biscuits unattended on her kitchen table. She hardly ever gets the couch all to herself. If she lingers in the bathtub, someone becomes impatient.

Elli loves the tub.

Katie and Elli take a break from working in the backyard pen.

Elli uses Katie's husband, Mike, as a stepstool to reach the remote.

"We have a big clawfoot soaking tub, and as soon as I get out in the morning and the water has drained, Elli jumps in and sits down as if it's her bath time," Katie says.

"She will sit there for quite a while, just relaxing."

Rushed baths are, for Katie, a minor inconvenience compared to the joy of living with Elli, her white Silkie city chicken.

Adopted from Chicken Run Rescue, Elli, like all Silkies, has blue skin and pouffy feathers that make her look like a miniature poodle. She and Katie's cat Juno seem to enjoy stirring up trouble together. They are the biscuit stealers—Juno knocks the food to the floor so Elli, who doesn't fly well enough to reach the tabletop, can feast alongside her. The two catch mice together. In the evenings, when Katie stretches out on the couch to watch TV, cat and hen, occasionally joined by Katie's other cat, Luna, settle on her chest and fall asleep. "Of course moving them is out of the question, since I get some pretty severe backtalk if I do."

Elli and Juno guard their territory well. Katie helps Mary and Bert by providing foster care for guests when Chicken Run Rescue has run out of room. If the foster chickens venture

Wings: Ginna

indoors, Elli and Juno rush over to "patrol" them—not to hurt them, but to let them understand who rules the roost.

In previous years, Chicken Run Rescue averaged around forty guests a year. From April 2009 to December 2010, they received inquiries to help 539 seized or surrendered chickens. Even with Katie, the Tallens, and several other foster caregivers pitching in, there aren't always enough spots for every bird in need.

Why the increase? Because urban flocks are on the rise. City dwellers concerned about where their food comes from decide to bypass supermarket eggs in favor of eggs gathered right in their backyard. But not everyone who raises city chickens is prepared for the work that goes into taking care of animals. Or they purchase chicks thinking they are hens, and one or two—or all—turn out to be roosters. And so Mary and Bert get another call. And another and another.

Mary used to paint and draw regularly. Over the years she has created beautiful, haunting portraits, shown in galleries as far away as London, England, of some of the birds she has been privileged to know. With so many chickens now in need, she rarely has time for art anymore. Neglecting her artistic side saddens her, but she sticks to her priorities. "The world will survive if I never do another painting, but if we don't take in a chicken, it could mean the difference between life and death for an animal."

An animal such as Miss Manor.

Katie and a foster hen.

Mary gives adopters a tour of Chicken Run Rescue.

TO THE
RESCUE . . .
AGAIN

So far they had made three unsuccessful trips to the Friendly Manor apartment complex in northeast Minneapolis to search for her. With temperatures forecast to drop below zero every night that week, they needed to find her. Fast.

Mary was away on jury duty when Bert received a noontime call from Friendly Manor's manager. She had spotted the black hen roosting in a juniper bush next to the building. Bert hung up the phone and raced to the car.

Wading through snow drifts, Bert cautiously approached the bush. The hen, whom Mary and Bert had been calling Miss Manor, panicked and flew over a low fence, landing at the base of a pine tree. The manager blocked Miss Manor's access back to the juniper bush while Bert crept toward her with a long pole net. Deep, powdery snow hampered the hen's movement. Down came the net.

Friendly Manor residents held open the building's front and back doors so Bert, his hand over Miss Manor's eyes to calm her, could more easily carry her to the parking lot. A blanket-covered pet carrier awaited. Earlier Mary had padded the bottom of the carrier with shredded paper to make it more comfortable on the hen's frostbitten feet.

Where had Miss Manor come from? A ragged piece of twine tied to her left leg suggested that, wherever it was, it was not a nice place. According to Mary, "That's a common way to 'keep' chickens without having to bother with providing any shelter. Just shackle them to a fence or any old piece of junk in your yard."

But from the moment of her capture, Miss Manor's life changed.

Now she would have a warm place to sleep, fresh food and water, plenty of space to explore. Now Bert would hold her and hum softly while Mary attended to her wounds.

Despite diligent antibiotic soaks, the leg that had been tied with rope was too damaged by frostbite to save. Yet the day after the amputation surgery, Miss Manor was up walking around the kitchen on her snazzy purple cast.

Mary says, "Miss Manor will stay with us for good, as all special needs birds do, but she'll do fine. We'll see that she has everything she needs and wants."

Come spring, whoever stops to peer through the peephole will be rewarded with a view of Miss Manor and her friends pecking, scratching, running, preening, nesting, or bathing in the dirt. For Mary and Bert, that's the best sight there is—the sight of chickens being chickens.

Bert holds Miss Manor during her initial examination back at Chicken Run Rescue.

MARY'S ART

To see more of Mary's artwork and read an interview with her, go to www.mnartists.org/article.do?rid=144657.

AUTHOR'S NOTE

My first visit to Chicken Run Rescue, in the fall of 2007, was supposed to be all business. Already sure I wanted to write a book about this intriguing place I'd discovered through an article in the *Minneapolis Star Tribune,* I brought along my tape recorder and a long list of interview questions. I was the picture of an impartial nonfiction author in action.

But, while trying to talk to Mary as she showed me around the yard, I found myself getting distracted.

Distracted by a hen named Olive repeatedly leaping up to snatch raisins from my laughing daughter's hand.

Distracted by Pa Zsa Zsa, whose malformed "scissor beak"—the top and bottom didn't align parallel, but crossed, like an open pair of scissors—made it challenging for her to eat. Still, she attacked heads of romaine lettuce with gusto.

Distracted by Bing, an inquisitive rooster who had nearly died from a recent infection. Mary recounted how she'd spent night after night sitting up with Bing, administering medication, and now here he was, briskly following us from pen to pen, pecking at the metal eyelets on my running shoes.

A few months later I read Mary's latest "Adoption Chronicles" newsletter for research and kept returning to the profile of a white crested black polish bantam hen named Kandinsky. Sporting the feathery afro of all crested chickens, Kandinsky crowed and had tiny leg spurs, so Mary and Bert assumed she was a rooster up until they found her first egg. Her former flock picked on her, leading her owner to surrender her to the Humane Society. Mary wrote that, ideally, Kandinsky should have a home "with no other birds or very docile ones."

Before long, Kandinsky had that home—my home. With a playpen serving as her coop, Kandinsky took up residence in the laundry room—and in the study and the kitchen and my daughters' bedrooms. We adopted her in February, when it was too cold for her to go outside, so we let her roam the house during the day. Once my oldest daughter sat down to practice piano

Kandinsky soaks up the sun.

Yeti dust-bathing

The author relaxing in the yard with Yeti and Kandinsky.

and kicked an egg resting against the pedals. If we went out to dinner and forgot to put Kandinsky in her playpen first, we'd come home to find her sleeping amid a pile of stuffed animals. Sometimes she'd duck behind the computer desk or hop upstairs, but we never worried about losing track of her. She chattered constantly in what Mary had accurately described as "soft little pips and squeaks so you can find her easily, like a little Geiger counter."

A few months later we adopted Yeti, the sweetest, gentlest rooster on the planet. He was a silkie, and, with his puffy white feathers and Kandinsky's crest, the two made a comical pair. When they were out in the backyard, confused passersby would stop to admire our "dogs." My husband and I set up an outdoor pen for them but always brought them back in the laundry room at night. (The laundry room is in the basement, right beneath my oldest daughter's bedroom. She eventually learned to sleep through five a.m. crowing.)

In the "Reasons to Adopt Chickens as Companion Animals" section on Chicken Run Rescue's website, Mary writes, "Chickens are highly intelligent, gentle, vivacious individuals who form strong bonds with each other as well as other species." I know from personal experience that this is absolutely true.

I also know what pure happiness looks like. It looks like Yeti flopping around in his dust bath under the hollyhocks, dirt flying every which way. It looks like Kandinsky lying on her side, eyes closed, wings extended over the grass or the concrete, basking in the sun.

Yeti and Kandinksy sunning themselves.

HOW TO CARE FOR CITY CHICKENS

A new guest is quarantined in the shower stall for a while before moving downstairs to join the rest of the flock.

Make sure it is legal to have chickens in your community. Check with your city government to see if you must apply for a permit or obtain neighbor approval.

Be prepared to keep your chickens for their entire life span. A chicken can live as long as a dog or a cat—fourteen years or more—though a hen's egg-laying slows down after the age of eighteen months and ceases by age three or four.

Chickens are descended from tropi-

cal jungle fowl, and thus are most comfortable in warmer weather, at temperatures between 55 and 75 degrees Fahrenheit. If you live in a climate where winter temperatures drop below freezing, you need to provide your flock with shelter that is insulated, moisture-proof, and adequately heated. It's not true, as many people believe, that a single light bulb is an acceptable heat source for a wintering flock.

Your chickens will need plenty of space to be happy. Allow four square feet of useable floor space per bird inside the coop and ten square feet of useable floor space per bird in an outdoor pen.

Outdoor coops must be solid enough to protect chickens from predators such as raccoons, dogs, possums, coyotes, hawks, and other animals that could view your flock as an easy meal. You can—and should—let your chickens roam in a fenced yard, but watch them closely. A loose dog slipping through an open gate can kill a chicken in seconds.

Plan to spend at least an hour a day feeding, playing with, and cleaning up after the birds. Buy good-quality chicken feed and supplement it with fresh fruits and vegetables—whatever your chickens like best, except for avocados, onions, and potato peels, which can be toxic to them. Use scratch (cracked corn and other seeds) only as a treat, not as a main food source.

Like all companion animals, chickens should be taken to the veterinarian when they are sick or hurt. Know which vets in your area will accept chicken patients.

Adopt birds from a reputable animal shelter instead of purchasing them from a hatchery or feed store.

For more information on city chicken care, visit Chicken Run Rescue's website: www.brittonclouse.com/chickenrunrescue.

Another cozy enclosure built by Mary and Bert.

FOR EDUCATORS

Alternatives to School Hatching Projects

According to Mary and Bert's friend Karen Davis, president of United Poultry Concerns, "Hatching projects encourage the view that animals are disposable objects instead of beings requiring a lifetime of care and commitment. They encourage children to want to bring more baby animals into the world, like litters of puppies and kittens no one wants when they grow up." Because mechanical incubators often malfunction or are not operated correctly, many classroom chicks are born sickly or deformed. If schools don't seek veterinary treatment for these animals, students get the impression that their well-being is not important.

Davis, in collaboration with education and animal welfare organizations, has put together a guide called Hatching Good Lessons, which includes a variety of activities that teach elementary school children about the life cycle of chickens and other birds without requiring live animals in the classroom. To order the guide or find a sampling of activities, visit www.upc-online.org/hatching/alternatives on the United Poultry Concerns website.

Feeding a raisin.

Mary and Bert's dog, Marco, with Hannah, the hen.

AUTHOR'S SOURCES

Davis, Karen. *Prisoned Chickens, Poisoned Eggs: An Inside Look at the Modern Poultry Industry*, revised edition. Summertown, Tenn.: Book Publishing Company, 2009.

Foer, Jonathan Safran. *Eating Animals*. New York: Back Bay Books, 2010.

Luttman, Gail and Rick. *Chickens in Your Backyard: A Beginner's Guide*. Emmaus, Pa.: Rodale, 1976.

Porter, Cynthya. "Baby Roosters Stolen from SMU," *Winona Daily News*, April 8, 2008, p. 1A.

Smith, Page, and Charles Daniel. *The Chicken Book*. Athens: University of Georgia Press, 2000.

Chicken Run Rescue:
www.chickenrunrescue.org

United Poultry Concerns:
www.upc-online.org